The Chester Books of Madri[gals]

2. LOVE AND MARRIAGE

Edited by Anthony G. Petti

For Lydia

CONTENTS

A selection of madrigals chosen from
The Chester Books of Madrigals
has been recorded by The Scholars on Accento ACR101
(Cassette ACT101)

CHESTER MUSIC

Cover:
May (Taurus/Gemini) from the
Très Riches Heures du Duc de Berry.
Reproduced by kind permission of the Musée Condé, Chantilly.

1. MON COEUR SE RECOMMANDE A VOUS

My heart commends itself to you, full of weariness and a martyr's pain, less to show you that it is free from jealousy than to gain strength to say goodbye. My lips, which were accustomed to smile for you and tell a pleasing tale, can now only curse those who banished me from your eyes. (Clément Marot)

Anonymous
attrib. Orlandus Lassus (1532-1594)

10

- ty - re; Au moins en dé - pit des ja - loux, Fai - tes qu'a - dieu

- ty - re; Au moins en dé - pit des ja - loux, Fai -

- ty - re; Au moins en dé - pit des ja - loux,

- ty - re; Au moins en dé - pit des ja - loux,

10

mp p p

15
[Fine]
vous puis - se di - [re, puis - se di] - re.
- tes qu'a - dieu vous puis - se di - - - re.
Fai - tes qu'a-dieu vous puis - se di - - re.
Fai - tes qu'a - dieu vous puis se di - re.
15
Fine
p
p
20
Ma bou - che qui vous sou - lait ri - - re, Et con - ter pro - pos
Ma bou - che qui vous sou - lait ri - - re, Et con - ter pro - pos
Ma bou - che qui vous sou - lait ri - - re, Et con - ter pro - pos
Ma bou - che qui vous sou - lait ri - re, Et con - ter pro - pos
poco più mosso
mp
ritmico
20
25
[D.C. al Fine]
gra - ci - eux, Ne fait main - te - nant que mau - di - re Ceux qui m'ont ban - ni de vos yeux.
gra - ci - eux, Ne fait main - te - nant que mau - di - re Ceux qui m'ont ban - ni de vos yeux.
gra - ci - eux, Ne fait main - te - nant que mau - di - re Ceux qui m'ont ban - ni de vos yeux.
gra - ci - eux, Ne fait main - te - nant que mau - di - re Ceux qui m'ont ban - ni de vos yeux.
poco meno mosso
25
mf
p
D.C. al Fine

2. COME AGAIN

John Dowland (1562-1626)

* Verse 3: poco più mosso.

+ Verse 3, last time: *cresc.*

3. SO WÜNSCH ICH IHR

So I bid her goodnight a hundred thousand times. If I consider her love all my misery disappears. When I see her she delights me; she has taken my heart prisoner, so that it burns and I cannot forget her.

20
(♯)
-freut sie mich, er - freut sie mich; sie hat mein Herz be - ses -
-freut sie mich, er - freut sie mich; sie hat mein Herz be - ses -
(♯)
-freut sie mich, er freut sie mich; sie hat mein Herz be - ses -
-freut sie mich; sie hat mein Herz be - ses - -
20
mf
25
- sen, drum ich num in dem Her - zen brinn, und
- sen, drum ich num in dem Her - zen brinn, und
- sen, drum ich num in den Her - zen brinn, und
- sen, drum ich num in den Her - zen brinn, und
25
mp
p
30
kann ihr nicht ver - ges - sen.
kann ihr nicht ver - ges - sen, und kann ihr nicht ver - ges - sen.
kann ihr nicht ver - ges - sen, und kann ihr nicht ver - ges - sen.
kann ihr nicht ver - ges - - sen, und kann ihr nicht ver - ges - - sen.
30
poco a poco dim.
rall.

4.MAS VALE TROCAR

Refrain. It is better to exchange pleasure for grief than to live without love.
1. Where it is honoured, dying is sweet; to live in oblivion is not to live at all.
   It is better to endure pain and grief than to live without love.
2. It is a lost life to live without love; that life is better which knows how to use love.
   It is better to suffer and feel pain than to live without love.
3. Love which has no suffering cannot please, because it has too little desire.
   It is better to lose pleasure on account of grief than to live without love.

5.SOSPIRAVA IL MIO CORE

My heart has been sighing as an escape from grief to imply that the soul can revive when my Lady (even she) will breathe a sigh that seems to say: "Don't die, please don't die".

15
-spir che di - cea: "L'a - ni - ma spi - ro!" Quan - do la Don-na mia più
-spir che di - cea: Quan - do la Don - na mia più
-spir che di - cea: "L'a - ni - ma spi - ro!" Quan - do la Don - na mia più
-spir che di - cea: Quan - do la Don - na mia più
-spir che di - cea: Quan - do la Don - na mia più
15
mp
mf
20
d'un so - spi - ro An - che el - la, an - che el - la so - spi - rò che pa -
d'un so - spi - ro An - che el - la, an - che el - la so - spi - rò che pa - rea di - re:
d'un so - spi - ro An - che el - la, an - che el - la so - spi - rò che pa - rea
d'un so - spi - ro An - che el la, an - che el - la so - spi-rò che pa - rea di - re, che pa -
d'un so - spi - ro An - che el - la so - spi - rò che pa - rea
20
p
mf
mp
mp
mp

25
30
-rea di - re, che pa-rea
"Non mo-rir, non mo-ri - - - re", che pa-
di - re: "Non mo-rir, non mo-ri - re", che pa-
- rea di - re: "Non mo - rir, non mo - rir, non mo - ri - re", che pa-rea di-
di - re: "Non mo - rir, non mo-ri - re", che pa - rea
mp
35
di - re: "Non mo-rir, non mo-ri - re, non mo - rir, non mo - ri - re!"
rea di - re: "Non mo - rir, non mo - ri - re, non mo - rir, non mo - ri - re!"
- rea di - re: "Non mo-rir, non mo-ri - - re!"
- re: "Non mo-rir, non mo-rir, non mo-ri - - re!"
di - re: "Non mo-rir, non mo - rir, non mo - ri - re!"
mf
f
poco rall.
A good copy is a purchased copy.

6. BACI SOAVI E CARI

Sweet and tender kisses, life-giving food to me, stealing my heart and then giving it back to me: you must learn how a ravished soul does not feel the pain of death but still it dies. How much sweetness there is in love; and therefore I always have kisses for you, O most delicious rosy lips, for in you there is total serenity. And if I were able to obtain your kisses, my life would end in so sweet a death.

Claudio Monteverdi (1567-1643)

Canto — Sop. (1)
Alto — Mezzo
Quinto — Alto
Tenore — Tenor
Basso — Bass

Allegretto 𝅗𝅥 = c. 60

Sop. (1): Ba - ci soa - vi e ca - ri, Ci - bi del - la mia vi - ta, C'hor — m'in - vo - la - te hor mi — ren - de - te il co - - re,

Mezzo: Ba - ci soa - vi e ca - ri, Ci - bi del - la mia vi - ta, C'hor — m'in - vo - la - te hor mi ren - de - te il co - re, Per voi con -

Alto: Ba - ci soa - vi e ca - ri, Ci - bi del - la mia vi - ta, C'hor m'in - vo - la - te hor mi ren - de - te il co - - re, Per voi con -

Tenor: Ba - ci soa - vi e ca - ri, Ci - bi del - la mia vi - ta, C'hor m'in - vo - la - te hor mi ren - de - te il cor - - re, Per voi con -

Bass: Per voi con -

15
Non sen -
- vien ch'im - pa - ri, co - me un' al - ma ra - pi - ta, e
- vien ch'im - pa - ri, co - me un' al - ma ra-pi - ta, Non
- vien ch'im - pa - ri, co - me un' al - ma ra - pi - ta, Non
- vien ch'im - pa - ri, co - me un' al - ma ra - pi - ta, Non
15
mp
mf
mf
20
- ta il duol di mor - t'e pur si mo -
pur si mor - re, e
sen - ta il duol di mor - te e pur
sen - ta il duol di mor - te e
sen - ta il duol
20
mf

25
- re, e pur si mo - re. Quan - t'ha di dol -
pur si mo - - - re. Quan - t'ha di dol -
si mo - re, si mo - re. Quan - t'ha di dol -
pur si mo - re, si mo - re. Quan - t'ha di dol -
e pur si mo - - re.
mf
25
p
mf
30
- c'a - mo - re! Per - chè sem-pr'io vi ba - ci, O
- c'a - mo - re! Per - chè sem-pr'io vi ba - ci, O
- c'a - mo - re! Per - chè sem - pr'io vi ba - - ci, O
- c'a - mo - re! Per - chè sem - pr'io vi ba - ci, O
O
30
mf
pp

35
dol - cis - si-mi ro - se! In voi tut - to ri - po - se. E s'io po-tessi à i vo - stri dol -
dol - cis - si-mi ro - se! In voi tut - to ri - po - se. E s'io po-tessi à i vo - stri dol -
dol - cis - si-mi ro - se! In voi tut - to ri - po - se. E s'io po-tessi à i vo - stri dol -
dol - cis - si-mi ro - se! In voi tut - to ri - po - se. E s'io po-tessi à i vo - stri dol -
dol - cis - si-mi ro - se! In voi tut - to ri - po - se.
mp
40
45
- ci ba - ci, La mia vi - ta fi - ni - re: O
- ci ba - ci, La mia vi - ta fi - ni - re: O
- ci ba - ci, La mia vi - ta fi - ni - re: O
- ci ba - ci, O
p
pp

50
che dol - ce mo - ri - - re, O che dol - ce
che dol - ce mo - ri - - re, O che dol - ce mo -
che dol ce mo - ri - - re, O che dol - ce mo - ri -
8
che dol - ce mo - ri - - re, O che dol - ce mo -
O che dol - ce mo -
50
mp
55
mo - ri - re! E s'io po - tessi à i vo - stri dol - ci ba -
- ri - - - re! E s'io po - tessi à i vo - stri dol - ci ba - ci,
(♭)
- - - - re! E s'io po - tessi à i vo - stri dol - ci ba - ci,
8
- ri - - - re! E s'io po - tessi à i vo - stri dol - ci ba - ci,
- ri - - - re!
55
p

60
- ci, La mia vi - ta fi - ni - re: O che dol - ce mo -
La mia vi - ta fi - ni - re: O che dol - ce mo -
La mia vi - ra fi - ni - re: O che dol - ce mo -
La mia vi - ta fi - ni - re: O che dol - ce mo -
La mia vi - ta fi - ni - re:
p>
p
mf
65
70
- ri - re, O che dol - - - ce mo - ri - re!
- ri - re, O che dol - ce mo - ri - - - re!
- ri - re, O che dol - ce mo - ri - re!
- ri - re, O che dol - ce mo - ri - - re!
O che dol - ce mo - ri - - - re!
molto dim. e rall.
f
pp

7. AU JOLI BOIS

Refrain. I shall skip off to the lovely woods.
1. My mum and dad have vowed to marry me off in six weeks.
2. In six weeks I'll be married to an old fellow that I shall deceive.
3. An old fellow that I shall deceive: I'll send him off to Cornouailles.

Charles Tessier(c.1550-?)

4. Droit en Cornuaille
   Je l'envoyerai,
   Et de ses richesses
   Largesse en ferai.
   Au joli bois.

5. Et de ses richesse
   Largesse en ferai
   A un beau jeune homme
   Je les donnerai.
   Au joli bois.

6. A un beau jeune homme
   Je les donnerai.
   S'il dit quelque chose,
   Je le gratterai.
   Au joli bois.

7. S'il dit quelque chose,
   Je le gratterai.
   Puis nous en irons
   Droit au bois jouer.
   Au joli bois.

4. I'll send him off to Cornuailles and take all his money.
5. I'll take all his money and give it to a sexy young man.
6. I'll give it to a sexy young man. If he says anything I'll scratch him.
7. If he says anything I'll scratch him. Then we'll go off to the woods to play.

8. MOTHER, I WILL HAVE A HUSBAND

Thomas Vautor (fl.1600-1620)

15
Dun should have had me long ere this, He said I had good lips to kiss, to kiss, to kiss, he said I had good lips to
Dun should have had me long ere this, He said I had good lips to kiss, to kiss, to kiss, he said I had good lips to
Dun should have had me long ere this, He said I had good lips to kiss, to kiss, to kiss, to
Dun should have had me long_ere this, He said I had good lips to__ kiss, to kiss, to
Dun should have had me long ere this, He said I had good lips to kiss, to kiss, to
15
mp
20
kiss, mo-ther, I will sure have one, In spite of her that will have none. For I have heard 'tis-trim, 'tis__
kiss, mo-ther, I will sure have one, In spite of her that will have none. For I have
kiss, mo-ther, I will sure have one, In spite of her that will have none. For I have heard 'tis trim, For
kiss, mo-ther, I will sure have one. For I have heard 'tis
kiss, mo-ther, I will sure have one, In spite of her that will have none. For I have
20
mp

25
trim, for I have heard 'tis trim, for I have heard 'tis trim when folks do love: By good Sir John I swear now I will
heard 'tis trim 'tis trim, for I have heard 'tis trim when folks do love: By
I have heard 'tis trim, for I have heard 'tis trim when folks do love: By good Sir John I swear now I will
trim, 'tis trim, for I have heard 'tis trim when folks do love: By good Sir John now I will
heard 'tis trim when folks do love: By good Sir John I swear now I will
25
mf
30
prove, now I will prove, by good Sir John I swear, now I will prove,
good Sir John I swear now I will prove, by good Sir John I swear, now I will prove,
prove, by good Sir John now I will prove, by good Sir John I swear, now I will prove; For,
prove, now I will prove, I by good Sir John I swear now I prove; For,
prove, now I will prove, by good Sir John I swear, now I will prove; For,
30
cresc.
mf
p

* Bar 42, Alto: the original reads G B B B D D D.

45
50
hus-band good or bad, to get me a hus - band good or bad. Mo-ther, I will have a hus-band, And I will have him out of hand,
hus-band good or bad, to get me a hus - band good or bad. Mo-ther, I will have a hus-band, And I will have him out of hand,
hus-band good or bad, to-get me a— hus - band good or bad. Mo-ther, I will have a hus-band, And I will have him out of hand,
hus-band good or bad, to get me a— hus - band good or bad. Mo-ther, I will have a hus-band, And I will have him out of—hand,
hus-band good or bad, to get me a hus - band good or bad. Mo-ther, I will have a hus-band, And I will have him out of hand,
poco rall.
I° tempo
* The original has ♩ ♩ for ♩. ♪ (cf. bar 3).
55
Mo-ther, I will sure have one, have one, In spite of her that will, in-spite of her that — will — have — none.
Mo-ther, I will sure have one, have one, In spite of her, in-spite of her that — will, that will have none.
Mo-ther, I will sure have one, have one, In spite of her, — in-spite of her that will have none.
Mo-ther, I will sure have one, have one, In-spite of her that will, in-spite of her that will have none.
Mo-ther, I will sure have one, In spite of her — that will have none.
cresc.
poco rall.
+ The original reads "lave".

9. ARISE, GET UP, MY DEAR

20
Hark, O hark, yon mer-ry, mer-ry mai-dens squeal - ing: spice-cake, sops in wine are now deal -
mer-ry, mer - ry mer-ry, mer - ry mai-dens squeal - ing: spice-cake, sops in wine, sops in wine are deal -
hark yon mer-ry, mer-ry wan-ton maid - - ens squeal - ing: spice-
25
- ing, spice-cake, sops in wine, sops in wine, sops in wine are a - - deal - ing, spice -
- ing, spice-cake, sops in wine sops in wine are deal - ing, spice-cake sops in wine, O fine
- cake, sops in wine, spice-cakes are a - deal - - ing, spice-cake, sops in wine,
30
35
- cake, sops in wine, sops in wine are now a-deal - ing: Run then, run a-pace, run a - pace, run
spice - cake, sops in wine, O fine, are a - deal - ing: Run then, run a-pace, run a-pace, run a - pace, run then,
sops in wine are a-deal-ing, are a-deal - ing: Run then, run a-pace, run a - pace then, run
cresc.

* Bars 59 ii-iii and 68 iv - 69 i, Mezzo: the original reads "Hark, list".

60
hark yon min-strels, how fine they firk it; And how the maids jerk it, With Kate and Will, Tom and Gill,
min-strels, how fine they firk it, firk it; And see how the maids jerk it, jerk it, With Kate and
min-strels, how fine they firk it; And how the maids jerk it, With Kate and Will, Tom and Gill, Hey ho,
60
p
p
65
Now a skip, Then a trip, fine-ly set a loft, There a-gain as oft, O bless-ed ho-li - day! List, hark yon
Will, and Gill, Now a trip, Then a skip, fine-ly set a - loft, Hey ho, fine brave ho - li - day! List, hark yon min-strels,
brave, Now a skip, Then a trip, fine-ly set a-loft On a fine wed-ding, wed - ding day! List, hark yon min-strels
65
cresc.
p
70
min-strels, how fine they firk it, And how the maids jerk it, With Kate and Will, Tom and Gill, Now a skip,
how fine they firk it, firk it, And see how the maids jerk it, jerk it, With Kate and Will, and Gill,
how fine they firk it, And how the maids jerk it, With Kate and Will, Tom and Gill, Hey ho, brave, Now a
70
p
p
cresc.

10. LEAVE OFF, HYMEN

Thomas Ravenscroft (c.1582-c.1635)

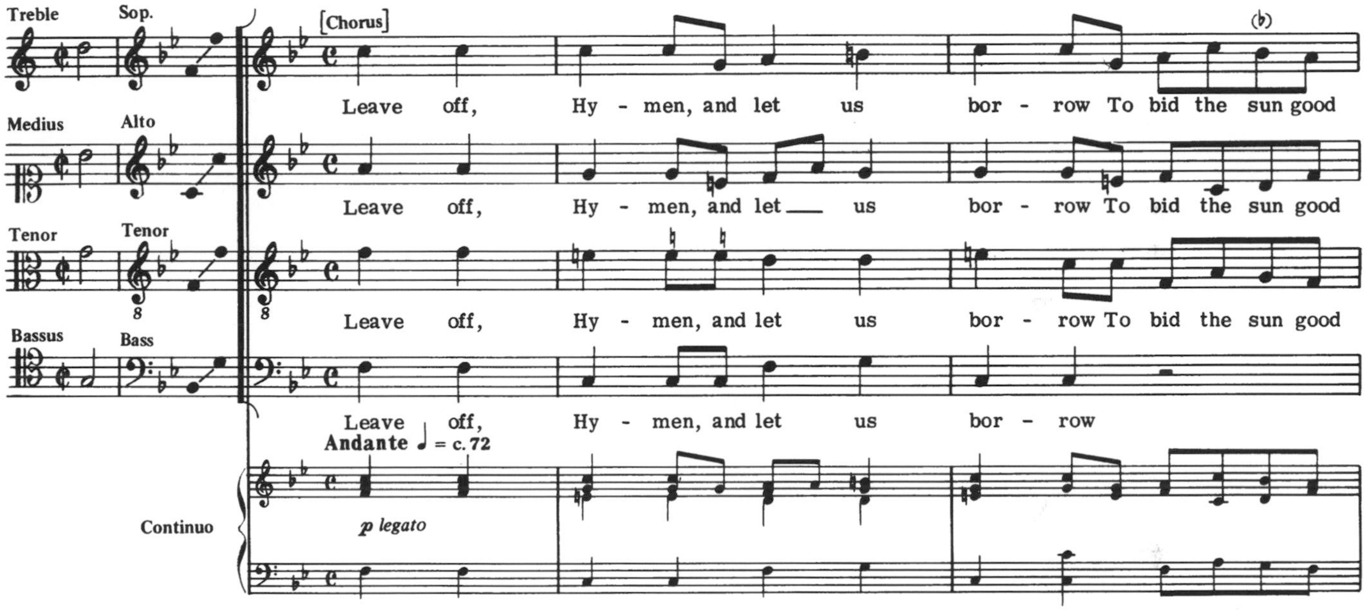

Treble / Sop.
Medius / Alto
Tenor / Tenor
Bassus / Bass

[Chorus]

Leave off, Hy - men, and let us bor - row To bid the sun good mor - row, good mor - row, *good mor - row,* good mor - row.

Leave off, Hy - men, and let us bor - row To bid the sun good mor - row, *to bid the sun good* mor - row, good mor - row, *good mor - row,* good mor - row.

Leave off, Hy - men, and let us bor - row To bid the sun good mor - row, *to bid the sun good mor - row,* good mor - row, *good mor - row,* good mor - row.

Leave off, Hy - men, and let us bor - row To bid the sun good mor - row, good mor - row, good mor - row, good mor - row.

Andante ♩ = c.72

Continuo

p legato

mp

rall.

5

[Fine]

Fine

Verse
See the sun can - not re - frain, But doth rise and give a - gain That which
*[ah]
*[ah]
*[ah]
tempo I [Solo]
mp
* The three lower parts may be taken by instruments or vocalised.
10
you of Hy-men bor - row, And with smil - ing bid'st good mor-row, good mor - row_To the sun, and to our
15
brides. Good - night to your sweet beau - ties, Sweet beau - ties touch your side.
[Da Capo]
poco a poco rall. e dim.
* E♭ in the original.
Da Capo

11. SCENDI DAL PARADISO

Come down from Paradise, O Venus, and bring your little cupids with you. May the graces and laughter be merrier than usual; beneath a serene sky may the Tiber bear to the Tyrrhenian Sea its horn adorned with pearls instead of water. And may our songs reach the stars, because the fair souls of Amaryllis and Thyrsis are united in the sacred and holy knot, as the vine to the elm, the ivy or acanthus to the trunk.

Luca Marenzio (1553-1599)

Canto / Sop. 1: Scen - di dal Pa - ra - di - so, Ve - ne - re, scen - di dal Pa - ra - di - so, Ve - ne - re, e te - co

Quinto / Sop. 2: Scen - di dal Pa - ra - di - so, Ve - ne - re, dal Pa - ra - di - so, Ve - ne - re, e te - co

Alto: dal Pa - ra - di - so, Ve - ne - re, dal Pa - ra - di - so, Ve - ne - re, scen - di dal Pa - ra - di - so, Ve - ne - r'e te - co -

Tenor: Scen - di dal Pa - ra - di - so, Ve - ne - re, scen-di, scen - di dal Pa - ra - di - so, Ve - ne - re,

Basso / Bass: Scen - di dal Pa - ra - di - so, Ve - ne - re, e te - co -

Andante 𝅗𝅥 = c. 66

mf mp

.... and rising prices ....

15
gui - da I par - go - let - ti A - mor: le gra - zie e'l
gui - da I par - go - let - ti A - mor: le gra - zie, le
gui - da I par - go - let - ti A - mor: le gra - zie e'l ri - -
I par - go - let - ti A - mor: le gra - zie e'l
gui - da I par - go - let - ti A - mor:
15
p
p
20
ri - - so Ol - tre l'u - sa - to ri - - - -
gra - zie e'l ri - - so Ol - tre l'u - sa - to ri - -
- so, e'l ri - - so Ol - tre l'u - sa - to ri - - - -
ri - so Ol - tre l'u - sa - to
e'l ri - so Ol - tre l'u - sa - to ri - - -
20
mf
p

25
da; In vi - sta il ciel se -
da; In vi - sta il ciel se -
dan; In vi - sta il ciel se - re -
ri - da, ri - da; In vi - sta il ciel se -
da;
25
p
30
re - no, Il Te - br'al mar' Tir - re -
re - no, Il Te - br'al mar' Tir - re -
no, Il Te - br'al mar' Tir - re -
re - no, Il Te - br'al mar' Tir - re -
Il Te - br'al mar' Tir - re -
30
mp
mp
Soon the music has to go out of print . . . .

35
-no Por - ti di per-le a - dor - no In - ve - ce d'ac-que'l cor - no.
- no Por - ti di per-le a - dor - no In - ve - ce d'ac-que'l cor - no.
- no Por - ti di per-le a - dor - no In - ve - ce d'ac-que'l cor - no.
- no Por - ti di per-le a - dor - no In - ve - ce d'ac-que'l cor - no. E i
- no E i
35
p
mp
40
E i no - stri can - ti giun - ga -
E i no - stri can - ti giun - ga - no a le stel - le
E i no - stri can - ti giun - ga - no a le stel -
no - stri can - ti, E i no - stri can - ti giun - ga - no a le stel -
no - stri can - ti, E i no - stri can - ti giun - ga-no a le
40

45
-no‿a le stel - le, giun - ga-no‿a le stel - - - - le, Poi -
giun - ga no‿a le, stel - le, giun - ga - no‿a le stel - - - - le, Poi -
- le, giun - ga-no‿a - le stel - - - le, Poi -
- le, e‿i no - stri can - ti giun - ga-no‿a le stel - le, Poi -
stel - - le,
45
50
- chè l'a - ni - me bel - le D'A -
- chè l'a - ni - me bel - - le
- chè l'a - ni - me bel - le D'A -
- chè l'a - ni - me bel - le D'A - ma-ril - li‿e di Tir - si
D'A - ma-ril - li‿e di Tir - si
50
55
.... and more fine works are lost from the repertoire.

60
- ma-ril - li e di Tir - si so - no u - ni - ti, d'A - ma-ril -
d'A - ma-ril - li e di Tir - si so - no u - ni - te,
- ma-ril - li e di Tir - si so - no u - ni - te, d'A - ma-ril - li e di Tir - si so - no u -
so - no u - ni - te, d'A - ma-ril - li e di Tir si,
so - no u - ni - te, d'A - ma-ril - li e di Tir - si so no u -
mp
60
mf
mp
mp
65
- li e di Tir - si, d'A - ma-ril - li e di Tir - si so - no u - ni -
d'A - ma - ril - li e di Tir - si, d'A - ma -ril - li e di Tir - si so - no u -
- ni - te, d'A - ma-ril - li e di Tir - si so - no u - ni - - - -
d'A - ma-ril - li e di Tir - si so - no u - ni - te
- ni - te, d'A - ma-ril - li e di Tir - si so - no u - ni -
65
mf
mf

* Two semibreves in the original.

* Alto and Tenor read "vita" in the original.

85
co - m'al tron-co l'e - de-ra o l'a - can - to, l'e - de-ra o l'a - can - to, O
tron- co l'e - de-ra o l'a - can - to, l'e - de-ra o l'a - can - to, O
co - m'al tron-co l'e - de-ra o l'a - can - to, l'e - de-ra o l'a - can -
co - m'al tron-co l'e - de-ra o l'a - can - to, l'e - de-ra o l'a - can - to,
O co - m'al tron - co
mp
85
f
90
co - m'al - tron - co l'e - de - ra o l'a - can - to.
co - m'al - tron - co l'e - de - ra o l'a - can - to.
- to, l'e - de-ra o l'a - can - to, l'e - de-ra o l'a - can - to.
O co - m'al tron - co l'e - de-ra o l'a - can - to.
l'e - de-ro a l'a - can - to, l'e - de-ra o l'a - can - to.
90
mf rall.
f
p

12. QUAND MON MARI VIENT DE DEHORS

When my husband comes rolling home, he pays me with a beating. He takes the spoon from the pot and hurls it at my head: I'm afraid he'll kill me. He's a lying, jealous wretch, a rotten old brawler and moaner. I'm young and he's old.

15
A la tête il me la ru - e, à la tête il me la ru - e: J'ai grand peur qu'il
A la tête il me la ru - e, à la tête il me la ru - e: J'ai grand peur qu'il
pot, A la tête il me la ru - e, à la tête il me la ru - e: J'ai grand peur qu'il
pot, A la tête il me la ru - e, à la tête il me la ru - e: J'ai grand peur qu'il
mf
f
p
20
ne me tu - e. C'est un faux vi - lain ja - loux, c'est un faux vi - lain ja - loux, c'est un vi - lain ri - o - teux, grom - me - leux. Je suis
ne me tu - e. C'est un faux vi - lain ja - loux, c'est un faux vi - lain ja - loux, c'est un vi - lain ri - o - teux, grom - me - leux. Je suis
ne me tu - e. C'est un faux vi - lain ja - loux, c'est un faux vi - lain ja - loux, c'est un vi - lain ri - o - teux, grom - me - leux. Je suis
ne me tu - e. C'est un faux vi - lain ja - loux, c'est un faux vi - lain ja - loux, c'est un vi - lain ri - o - teux, grom - me - leux. Je suis
ritmico
mf
f
mp
25
jeune et il est vieux: c'est un vi - lain ri - o - teux, grom - me - leux. Je suis jeune et il est vieux, je suis jeune et il est vieux.
jeune et il est vieux: c'est un vi - lain ri - o - teux, grom - me - leux. Je suis jeune et il est vieux, je suis jeune et il est vieux, et il est vieux.
jeune et il est vieux: c'est un vi - lain ri - o - teux, grom - me - leux. Je suis jeune et il est vieux, je suis jeune et il est vieux, et il est vieux.
jeune et il est vieux: c'est un vi - lain ri - o - teux, grom - me - leux. Je suis jeune et il est vieux, je suis jeune et il est vieux, et il est vieux.
p
mf
f
marcato

13. FIVE SEVENTEENTH CENTURY ROUNDS

(i) O MY LOVE

(ii) I LAY WITH AN OLD MAN

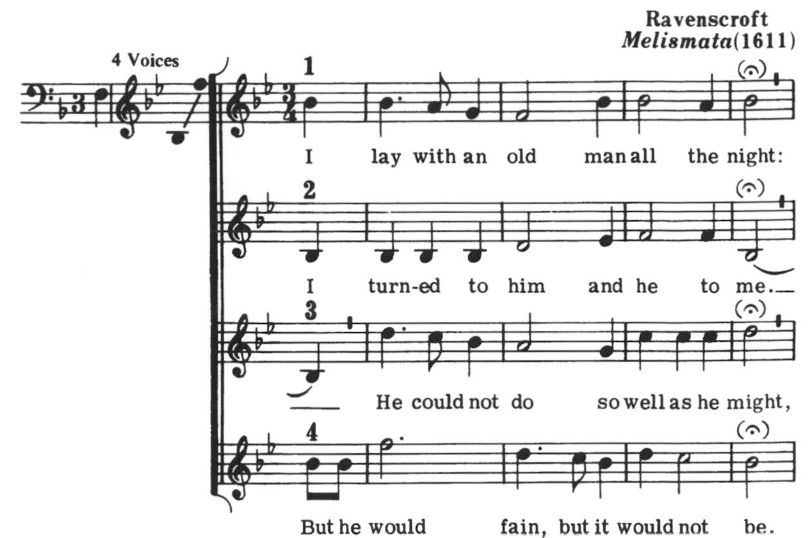

(iii) HEY HO, WHAT SHALL I SAY?

(iv) WHAT HAP HAD I?

2. From morn to e'en her tongue ne'er lies;
Sometime she brawls, sometime she cries,
Yet I can scarce keep her talons from my eyes.

3. If I go abroad and late come in,
"Sir knave," saith she, "where have you been?"
And do I well or ill, she claps me on the skin.

(v) WHENEVER I MARRY

EDITOR'S NOTES

1. General. This series is a thematic anthology of secular European madrigals and part-songs from the 16th and early 17th centuries. The settings are mainly for mixed four-part choir, but there are also some for three and five voices, and an occasional one for six. Five voices are strongly represented because this was an especially popular number in late 16th century madrigals. By and large, the items present relatively few vocal or harmonic difficulties for the fairly able choir, and where more than four parts are required, they are usually drawn from the upper voices (mainly the sopranos), with the tenor line hardly ever being split.

The term madrigal has been interpreted rather loosely. Besides the contrapuntal part-song, it relates to frottola, ayre, chanson, lied and the villancico, whether courtly or folk (these all basically being harmonised melodies, often very simply set, and usually repeated for each stanza). More obviously, it encompasses the ballet (a short stanzaic setting with repeats and fa la las), and the canzonet (a lighter style madrigal normally for a small number of voices). Rounds and catches have also been included because they were obviously an important component of a sing-song or a drinking party, certainly in 17th century England, and their choice of subject matter is very free-ranging. To help make madrigal concerts rather more of a party than a performance, at least two or three of the rounds in each volume have been selected as simple enough to be sung by an audience with or without a visual aid (see section 5, no. (v) of these notes).

One of the most important features of this anthology is the arrangement by subjects, each volume being devoted to one of the prevalent topics in secular songs, for example, "The Animal Kingdom" (vol. 1), "Love and Marriage" (vol. 2) and "Desirable Women" (vol. 3). This provides not only a new approach to madrigal anthologies but also, more importantly, a focus for the singers and, it is hoped, a comprehensible, appetising programme for the audience. Thus, it should be possible to provide a short concert entirely from one of these volumes, and two halves of a longer concert from any two.

Each volume contains at least twelve part-songs and, on average, half a dozen rounds. About one-third of the texts are in English, but an attempt has been made to provide a representative collection of Italian and French lyrics, and, to a lesser extent, of German and Spanish. The selection combines indispensable popular works with a fair mixture of relatively unfamiliar but attractive and singable pieces. Some thought has also been given to affording a balance between the lively and the reflective, the happy and the sad, for the sake of variety of mood and to help mirror the ups and downs, real or imagined, of Renaissance life and love.

2. Editorial method. As with the Chester Latin Motet series, the Editor has endeavoured to make the volumes suitable for both performance and study. The madrigals are transposed, where necessary, into the most practical keys for ease of vocal range, are barred, fully underlaid in modernised spelling and punctuation, are provided with breathing marks, and have a simplified reduction as a rehearsal aid or as a basis for a continuo. Editorial tempi and dynamics have been supplied, but only in the reduction, leaving conductors free to supply their own according to their interpretation, vocal resources and the acoustics. The vocal range is given at the beginning of each piece, as also are translations for the non-English texts.

To help musicologists, the madrigals are transcribed from the most authoritative sources available. Original clefs, signatures and note values are given at the beginning and wherever they change during the course of a piece. Ligatures are indicated by slurs, editorial accidentals are placed above the stave, and the underlay is shown in italics when it expands a ditto sign, or in square brackets when it is entirely editorial. Where the original contains a *basso continuo* it is included as the bass line of the reduction. Instrumental parts (which appear only occasionally in these volumes, e.g. Ravenscroft's *Leave Off, Hymen,* no. 10) are transcribed within the relevant vocal lines as well as in the reduction. Finally, each volume contains brief notes on the scope of the edition, the composers, stylistic features of the part-songs, and the sources used, while editorial emendations and changes are given in the footnotes within the text proper.

3. The themes and the lyrics. The predominant theme in 16th century lyrics is love. Most usually the love is unrequited and is nearly always depicted from the man's point of view. In the Petrarchan tradition, which carries through until the early 17th century, the mistress is a paragon of beauty and virtue, but incredibly aloof and seemingly cruel to her faithful swain, on whom she will scarcely waste a glance. Thus, there is a profusion of languishing laments often bordering on a romantic agony of contemplated suicide. Yet, clearly, the lover would instantly and magically recover if only he could gain a smile from the beloved. These self-pitying utterances acknowledge none of the old Roman virtue of *gravitas*; neither do they recognize any boundary of nationality. It should be noted, however, that the Italian imitators of Petrarch are usually the most effusive, certainly to judge from the texts of nos. 5 and 6, which were set by several different composers in the period. No. 5, for example, is in the panting and bleeding hearts tradition. For long, the heart has been considered the seat of the affections, though it is now being replaced by the stomach and the gut. The lover's heart in no. 5 does not require a transplant; a mere sigh from the Lady will suffice. In no. 6, the heart has been the victim of tender larceny, and requires for revival not simply a sigh, but numerous "kisses of life" for resuscitation. But in the paradoxical style which characterises so much Renaissance lyric poetry, the lover would gladly be kissed to death – a fate intended to be analogous to sexual consummation. Another poem in the heart tradition, but far more restrained, comes from the pen of the French lyric poet, Clément Marot (no. 1). The lover's heart is paying the mistress a courtesy farewell call. Any notion of sentimentality is carefully checked, though in the verse section there is a sad and bitter commentary that (moving to another part of the anatomy) the lips that once smiled can now only utter curses on those who caused the lovers to separate.

Yet another heart, this time a burning one, together with a more optimistic valediction, is contained in the German lyric, *So Wünsch Ich Ihr* (no. 3). The burning or the flaming heart was a very popular Renaissance and early Baroque emblem for both secular and sacred love (it was used by the Jesuits, among others, with the sigla I.H.S.). The emblem runs like a forest fire through madrigal verse, the most famous example from the English school being Thomas Morley's *Fire, Fire, My Heart,* which requires the services of a skilled fire brigade. The lover in the German lyric is far more tranquil, and is like a contented Romeo, bidding his mistress a somewhat lavish hundred-thousand goodnights, and passively voicing the paradox that his heart is best off when it is the Lady's prisoner.

In the English love lyric, *Come Again* (to spy a pun would be anachronistic), there is both a heightening and a control of the emotions through the skilful use of rhetoric and narrative sequence, the latter being more apparent in the original, which has six verses. All the usual flowers of rhetoric raise their pretty heads, including apostrophe, repetition, distribution and climactic sequence, especially in stanzas one and two. The lover's frustration is cleverly mirrored in the climaxes and culminates in the bitter realisation in the last stanza that the Lady laughingly exults in her conquest. The lyric also introduces a frequent visitor to the love madrigal, blind Cupid, who has successfully pierced the lover's heart, but can do nothing to the flinty-hearted mistress. The final English example of despairing love is the first of the rounds, *O My Love,* the words of which are brief and to the point: if you really love me, come quickly or you'll be the death of me. The Spanish poets can mope as much as the others, but the example here, *Mas Vale Trocar* (no. 4), is a more general and idealised statement, the constant refrain in this beautiful lyric being that it is better to live in pain and grief than to live without love.

In view of the general despondency in love poetry of the Renaissance (though there are brilliant exceptions, including the *Songs and Sonnets* of John Donne), it may appear surprising that anyone ever got married to the actual person desired. Still, most of the comedies of the period, including Shakespeare's, end with a set of appropriate weddings, usually accompanied with songs and dances. There are two examples of nuptial songs or prothalamia in this collection. The first is the splendid *Scendi Dal Paradiso* (no. 11), in which the words seem to echo prayers from the Nuptial Mass. Venus is invoked as if she were the Holy Spirit, and the pastoral images of union are faintly analogous to the Nuptial Blessing. The English example, *Leave Off, Hymen* (no. 10), is simpler but nevertheless very delicate. This time it is not Venus who is invoked but Hymen, the Greek god of marriage and son of Apollo. The sungod himself is also indirectly referred to, since the sun will be greeted with a happy "good morrow" after a night of nuptial bliss.

A far more naturalistic description of a wedding day is provided by the lively doggerel of *Arise, Get Up, My Dear* (no. 9). A sluggerbed and somewhat sad girl, possibly a bridal attendant, is urged to get out of bed to avoid being late for the wedding festivities, which include the consuming of spice-cake and sops in wine, and dancing to the music of a band with a good beat ("how fine they firk it"). Parts of the wedding rituals are mentioned, including the distributing of the gold bridal laces tied around sprigs of rosemary ("for fear of old snatching"—whatever that means).

A suitable companion for the reluctant girl of *Arise, Get Up, My Dear* is the petulant immature lass of no. 8, *Mother I Will Have A Husband* (a madrigal which used to signal the sudden departure of the unattached males from a singing group whenever an unattached female suggested it). Here we have a spirited defiance of parental authority: the girl wants a husband at all costs, if not John a Dun, who finds her lips very kissable, then anyone she can find in the big city. The lyric has a charming authenticity about it, and lends a distinct country flavour by contrast to the mainly courtly madrigals in this collection.

An equally rebellious but more calculating girl is the speaker in *Au Joli Bois* (no. 7). Her parents threaten to marry her off to a rich old man within six weeks. Though she cannot avoid this marriage of convenience, she will make capital out of it. "To the woods", she exclaims in a variant on the old familiar risqué joke. There she will find her boyfriend and eventually lavish on him all the old man's riches. A less resourceful French lady, another victim of a marriage of convenience, is wedded to an old man who is also a wife-beating drunkard in *Quand Mon Mari Vient De Dehors* (no. 12). The potentially serious situation is related almost in Punch and Judy style. The lyric ends in defiant rage, and one wonders whether the wife will eventually, in Browningesque fashion, help the old wretch on his way to the grave. The classic January and May situation is reflected in many of the songs of the period, and the second round in this collection, *I Lay With An Old Man,* concerns a woman's night-long vigil for satisfaction from an old man whose spirit is willing but whose flesh is weak.

The last three rounds deal with marriage from the man's point of view. In *Hey Ho, What Shall I Say,* the cuckolded husband feebly notes that Sir John (the English Don Giovanni?) has stolen his wife. But he is only moderately upset and reflects that she will return when she is ready. *What Hap Had I?* represents the traditional henpecked husband married to an untameable shrew. To make matters worse, she beats him. The man in the last round, *Whenever I Marry,* is extremely cautious: if he does marry he will choose a maiden and not a widow, for widows are headstrong and domineering. This crude generalisation highlights the fact that only in widowhood did women have adequate property rights and a certain measure of independence, though this scarcely helped a Duchess of Malfi. Thus, in many ways, the part-songs of the period provide not only good music but also a remarkably comprehensive insight into literary and social history.

4. The composers and the music. The collection begins with a simple and tender chanson, *Mon Coeur Se Recommande A Vous,* which is sometimes ascribed, without evidence, to Lassus, who composed a fine five-part setting. It is especially unfortunate that neither the composer nor the source for this chanson is known, and the Editor's extensive search for it among the extant settings as listed in J. Rollin, *Les Chansons De Clément Marot,* Paris 1951 (especially pp. 205-6), proved unavailing. He has had to use a reconstruction, as all modern editors apparently have, which ultimately derives from the arrangement for solo voice and keyboard in Jean-Baptiste Weckerlin, *Echos Du Temps Passé,* Paris, 1853-7, vol.1, p.32. The chanson, framed in aba, has a haunting melody suggestive of Arcadelt, coupled with the rhythmic suppleness of Claude Le Jeune. The close harmony, which is mainly chordal, gives the melody warmth and breadth, and the short fugue which closes the refrain adds a plaintive poignancy. The verse section provides variety of mood in its slightly animato movement and acerbity in the C sharps, which sometimes imply D minor and provide an ambivalent A major final cadence. By the end of the verse the ear eagerly awaits the return to F major and the almost somnolent smoothness of the refrain.

John Dowland (1562-1626), the composer of *Come Again,* is one of the band of late Elizabethan composers who spent a considerable time travelling abroad. His first excursion led him to Paris, where he was in service with the English

Ambassador, Sir Edward Stafford. Around 1582, under the influence of Richard Verstegan and others, he became a Catholic, though he seems later to have recanted. His travels took him to Germany and then to Venice and Florence. He was always in great demand as a lutenist, holding this position for several years at the Danish Court (1598-1606) and eventually becoming court lutenist in England. In vocal music Dowland is best known for his books of ayres, mostly for solo voice and lute, though some he devised to be sung optionally for voices and viols *ad libitum.* Such a song is *Come Again,* which was published in *The First Booke of Songes and Ayres of Fowre Partes with Tableture for the Lute,* London, 1597 (copy in British Library). Clearly, the top line has all the melody and most of the fun, but the other parts are at least singable, and engage in an exciting little piece of syncopated antiphony with the soprano in the concluding section (bars 7-10). The piece is quite jaunty and shows bravura in dramatising what might otherwise be an overly serious lament. In particular, the last section, with its madrigalian use of quaver rests for the panting lover and its fine sense of sequential climax, provides a splendid equipoise of sweetness and bitterness and never loses its sense of lively tension.

Melchior Franck (c. 1580-1639) is one of the more prominent German composers of the early 17th century. He was also a singer and held the post of Kapellmeister at Coburg from 1603 to his death in that city. His music is quite varied in style and encompasses motets, chorales and a goodly number of secular lieder. He can be both very ornate and polychoral in the Venetian manner, or quite simple in a basic German vernacular style in which he is invariably tuneful and often mellifluous. *So Wünsch Ich Ihr* first appeared in Franck's *Musicalischer Bergkreyen In Welchen Allweg Der Tenor Zuworderst Intonirt In Contrapuncto Colorato Auf Vier Stimm Gesetzt,* 1602 (complete set of copies in the Staats-und Universitätsbibliothek, Hamburg). In keeping with the title-page, the song begins with a solo tenor voice, possibly sung against an accompaniment, though I have assumed a treatment similar to the old plainchant form of intonation, especially since the opening is conceived in a transposed Dorian mode. Thereafter, the modality and harmony take a number of unpredictable turns as they follow the connotations of the text, the progressions being smoothed by a large number of roulades in virtually all the parts, in a style reminiscent of string music. A most impressive expression of intensity in love, the piece requires very secure intonation and firm breath control to make the beauties of this reflective song fully apparent.

Juan del Encina was born in Salamanca in 1468 and died in Laón around 1530. He was not only the greatest composer of the secular villancico in his time, but also a man of many parts who gained considerable success as a playwright. While in the service of the Duke of Alba he was master of the revels and wrote both the text and the music for plays performed at court. He was ordained in 1519 and held ecclesiastical positions in Málaga and Laón. The main source for Encina compositions is the courtly song-book Cancionero de Palacio, a manuscript dating from 1500 in the Biblioteca de Palacio, Madrid (MS 1335), which includes the present one, *Mas Vale Trocar* (ff. 209v.-10). Like many Encina villancicos, it is short, rhythmically vital and haunting in its refrain. (Compare with the song-books of the reign of Henry VIII, which have somewhat similar qualities). As in the Dowland song, the music has a sprightliness which counterbalances rather than reinforces the idealistic seriousness of the words.

It will seem a trifle odd to include in an anthology on love and marriage a madrigal by a man who murdered his first wife and her lover, but why should not a composer, like his music, abound in paradox? Don Carlo Gesualdo was a Neopolitan who became Prince of Venosa. He improved his position, his wealth and his musical contacts by marriage to his second wife, Isabella d'Este, through whom he thus had access to the Ferrara circle, which included the poet Tasso. Gesualdo's relatively substantial body of music (including six volumes of madrigals and four volumes of sacred music) stands out for its often weird chromaticism and dissonance, unpredictable harmonies and violent changes of mood. Some musicologists explain the style simply as an outcome of his neurosis, much as El Greco is explained away by astigmatism, though both can be called mannerists. At all events, the music always seems to have integrity and preserves its own level. However, it is with reluctance that any cautious anthologist would include much of Gesualdo's work, since it is difficult to perform and can leave the average audience bemused. Nevertheless, the present work, *Sospiravi Il Mio Core,* is only of moderate difficulty and can be sustained without too much trouble. It was first published in *Madrigali Libro Terzo,* Ferrara, 1595, (first complete set of extant copies, 2nd edition, Venice 1607, housed in the Bibliothèque du Conservatoire National de Musique, Paris). The writing is quite exposed, with all five parts rarely used. Word-painting is present from the very beginning, with the familiar rests punctuating the syllables of such words as "sospirava". Suspensions abound, especially in words denoting grief and death, but chromaticism is uncharacteristically absent, even if the madrigal strangely gives the impression that it is there nonetheless. The fullest and most effective writing is reserved for the final section of this segmented madrigal, with the pattern of falling and then rising figures for "morir" and "morire", culminating in a slow suspension with all voices in the lower register. Tonally the work is not adventurous for Gesualdo, for it stays mainly within the confines of A minor and E minor.

The next madrigal, *Baci Soavi E Cari,* by Monteverdi (biographical details in Volume 1), comes close to ecstasy. An early work, it was first published in *Il Primo Libro de Madrigali,* Venice, 1587. No complete set of parts of this edition has survived, but the second edition of 1607 exists intact in the Civico Museo, Bologna. It is interesting to compare this early work with *Dolcissimo Usignolo* (vol. 1) from his last collection of madrigals. They are similar in romantic feeling, though the latter is a little more airy and delicate. In any case, it would be hard to suggest that Monteverdi lost his romanticism with age, witness the ravishing love duet from the *L'Incoronatione Di Poppaea.* Both madrigals are homophonic and even chordal; the sections are closed off, and the last section is repeated. Both use the bass sparingly and often concentrate attention on the three upper voices. Above all, they have ravishingly sweet melodic phrases which are highly sensitive to the connotations and speech-rhythms of the words.

The French composer, Charles Tessier, is still something of an unknown quantity. He was born near Montpellier around 1550, and although most of the rest of his life is a blank, he was apparently an established lutenist and composer, and toured with Henry IV of France as one of his chamber musicians. While in London he published his first collection of part-songs, *Premier Livre de Chansons et Airs de Court,* printed by William Byrd's publisher, Thomas

East, in 1597 (complete set of copies in the Bibliothèque Nationale, Paris). Like all the chansons in that collection, *Au Joli Bois* has a light, breezy, quasi-folk melody, and a simple, yet effective chordal accompaniment. The song contains a lively cyclic movement of refrain, verse, refrain, and perfectly fits the temperament of the wilful, defiant girl, with a characteristic laughing melisma for "bois".

Even more of a blur in terms of biography is Thomas Vautor, who flourished in the early 17th century and was in service with James I's favourite, the Duke of Buckingham. He published a solitary volume of madrigals, at a time when the form was rapidly dying out of fashion: *The First Set: Beeing Songs of Divers Ayres and Natures of Five and Sixe Parts: Apt for Vyols and Voices,* 1619 (set of copies in British Library). *Mother, I Will Have A Husband* is one of the brightest and dramatic of his madrigals, and is certainly more interesting than the best known piece in the collection, *Sweet Suffolk Owl,* though obviously not as lyrical. In particular, the fast speech-rhythms of the quavers brilliantly depict the empty-headed agitation of the importunate daughter and the patter of nonsense that streams from her ever open lips. The change of time from duple to six-four admirably conveys her sudden resolution to take action, and the jaunty gait of the passage almost implies her skipping off to town somewhat in emulation of Kemp's Jig.

It is hard to imagine a madrigal anthology without any of the works of the Prince of English madrigalists, Thomas Morley (1557-1602), the most distinguished pupil of William Byrd. As well as being a versatile composer, Morley was an excellent organist and held this post at St. Paul's Cathedral from 1592. He was made a Gentleman of the Chapel Royal in 1598. His output in madrigals and allied forms is formidable, though he wrote a fair amount of English and Latin sacred music too. *Arise, Get Up, My Dear* comes from the delightful collection with the tautologous title, *Canzonets. Or Little Short Songs to Three Voyces,* London, 1593 (copies in the British Library). The piece is masterly in the fullness of its three-part harmony and counterpoint and its range of invention. It begins with a slow rising fugue to pull the sleepy-head from her mattress, and then gathers speed and excitement as the bride comes into view. Quavers and a modulation to C major indicate the merry squeal of wanton maidens, and a stretto fugue provides a mix of cakes and wine-sops followed by syncopation for the exhortation to run to get a bride-lace. The joyful ritual of the rosemary branch is expressed in chordal triple time, and then the pace slows and the key moves momentarily in D minor for the sudden tears, quickly to be dispelled by the sound of the minstrels. The last section is a *tour de force* in representing the breathless jigging wedding dance, again in stretto fugue, with a quick, dotted and extremely tuneful figure, which Morley repeats but eventually brings to an exhausting halt. The merry confusion of the whole final section is reinforced by the marked differences in the text of each line, though it is chastening to think that these may not be the conscious intention of the composer but the incompetence of the typesetters.

In much quieter and more solemn mood is *Leave Off Hymen,* the little nuptial hymn of Thomas Ravenscroft (biographical details in vol. 1), which appears in his *Briefe Discourse,* 1614 (copy in British Library). The treatment is tender and the harmonies are subtle, for although the piece starts in Dorian mode, here transposed to G in the key of F, it moves frequently into the related keys of C major and F major. For best effect, strings should be used to accompany the solo voice and to double the chorus.

Luca Marenzio (1553-99) is to the Italian madrigal what Morley is to the English. In his youth he was a chorister at Brescia Cathedral, then served as musician and later choirmaster to Cardinal d'Este in Rome. A second great cardinal, Aldobrandini, gave him patronage and employment in 1594, and with them entry into a circle which included the poets Tasso and Guarini. Like several other Italian musicians (including Giovanni Francesco Anerio a little later), he spent a while at the Polish Court, but by the time of his death he was back in Rome. Marenzio composed a fairly substantial corpus of sacred music, including somewhat madrigalian motets (cf. *The First Chester Book of Latin Motets*), but his reputation rests mainly on his collection of five hundred madrigals, and has to be taken somewhat on trust, since relatively little of his work is performed or recorded as yet. To judge from *Scendi dal Paradiso,* his reputation is justly deserved. The madrigal is a mature work and was first published in *Il Quarto Libro De Madrigali,* Venice 1587 (complete set of copies in the Civico Museo, Bologna). An expansive work of grace and majesty, it contains a wide variety of tuneful themes which reflect the mood and meaning of the text. Word-painting is freely applied and is often quite complex, as may be seen from the very opening in which Marenzio achieves a triple effect in a remarkably brief span. The invocation begins in a dropping fugue of fifths for "Scendi", then all the parts move stepwise down the scale making a type of crystal stairway for the goddess. At the same time, the canon of "dal Paradiso" gives the impression of a silvery peal of bells, immediately setting the mood for a wedding celebration. Other examples of word-painting include the quick dotted melismas for laughter ("riso" and "ridan"), the extended dotted ascent to the stars ("giungano a le stelle"), and the undulating melismas for the vine ("la vite"). After all the variety of invention, the ending comes as something of an anticlimax in an otherwise brilliant work.

The final madrigal in this collection, by Orlandus Lassus (biographical details in vol. 1) is a comic statement of male brutality in marriage. Lassus, whose versatility knows no bounds, uses a suitably crude, jerky style with mainly chordal harmonies, so that the staccato force of the woman's complaint is not lost on the ear. Angular duets and frequent modulation (though to related keys) help depict the unease and tension of the speaker, but she emerges in triumph at the end, with a G major cadence emphasizing that since she is young and her husband old, the misery cannot last for ever.

The rounds in this volume are mainly by Thomas Ravenscroft. They serve to remind us (as Volume One does) of what a mine of tuneful popular material he provides, even if he did not compose it all. His rounds come in every shape and size and deal with a diversity of topics, which he often groups thematically. The selection here ranges from a simple three-part round to an ambitious nine-part, though in nearly every case each part is accommodated without melodic awkwardness. The three collections from which they are taken, *Pammelia* (1609), *Deuteromelia* (1609), and *Melismata* (1611), survive in the British Library and are available in facsimile. *O My Love* appears in Walsh's *Catch Club* (1762) in the minor key as well. The last round, *Whenever I Marry,* is possibly by William Lawes, though unascribed in the collection from which it is taken, John Hilton's *Catch That Catch Can,* 1652 (p. 85), also extant in the British Library and reprinted in facsimile. Hilton does for the middle of the 17th century what Ravenscroft does for the beginning, though in Hilton the rounds are usually more extended and sophisticated.

5. Notes on Programming. The performance of a concert according to themes can be augmented and enhanced in a number of ways. The following points are suggested by the Editor in the light of his experience in directing concerts for a general audience.

(i). Briefly introduce each item or groups of items, and highlight the salient stylistic features. For foreign madrigals it is useful to read or declaim a translation even if one is provided in the programme.

(ii). Include some solo items on the same theme. There are innumerable songs to chose from among the works of such composers as John Dowland (e.g., *Come Away, Sweet Love; If My Complaints; I Saw My Lady Weep*), Thomas Campian *(Love Me Or Not; Shall I Come Sweet Love; There Is A Garden In Her Face)*, Alfonso Ferrobosco *(I Am A Lover; Why Stays The Bridgroom ?)* and Giovanni Coperario (*While Dancing Rests* – another Hymen song). For comic relief there are songs like Ravenscroft's *Hodge Trillindle To His Zweet Hort Malkyn,* and the anonymous song of a henpecked husband, *Come Batchelors And Married Men* (W. Chappell, *Popular Music Of Olden Times,* repr. 1967, vol. 1). Ideas for English songs as also for other madrigals can be gleaned from the revised E. H. Fellowes, *English Madrigal Verse* (1967). There are, of course, several anthologies of Renaissance and Early Baroque songs, including one put out by Penguin; and the possibilities are almost endless in relation to Continental songs, though the Editor has a special predilection for the songs of Sermisy (e.g., *Tant Que Vivrai*) and Monteverdi (including possibly the loveliest of all Renaissance duets, *Chiome D'Oro*).

(iii). A concert can be filled out and given variety by introducing occasional readings from the drama, prose and poetry of the period, either to supplement or contrast with the madrigals. As always, Shakespeare provides a wealth of selections, e.g., the opening of *Twelfth Night* or Viola's "She never told her love" (II, iv); a passage from *Romeo and Juliet;* an exchange between Benedick and Beatrice in *Much Ado,* or between Rosalind and Orlando in *As You Like It.* For contrasts, the *Taming of the Shrew* is rich in material, the description of the wedding of Katharina and Petruchio being especially apt (III, ii). Useful prose readings on sundry topics can be found in such anthologies as J. Dover Wilson's *Life in Shakespeare's England* and M. St Claire Byrne's *The Elizabethan Home* and *Elizabethan Life in Town and Country.*

For Renaissance poetry, various anthologies are available to assist the search for readings, including the Oxford *Book of 16th Century Verse* (which contains such gems as Drayton's *Since there's no help*) and the *Oxford Book of 17th Century Verse* (with a good selection from the Metaphysicals and the brief, pragmatic *Why so pale and wan ?* by Suckling. Similar anthologies are put out by Penguin Books, and among the collections related to the themes in this volume are the *Faber Book of Love Poetry* and the *Everyman Book of English Love Poems.* There is even an *Anthology of Erotic Verse,* edited by Derek Parker.

(iv). If conditions allow, a cyclorama or screen can be employed as a backdrop for slides from works of art roughly contemporaneous with the pieces performed, assuming there are no problems with copyright. Renaissance art is crowded with paintings of lovers, courtships, weddings and family groups from every country and every school of painting. Of the many guides to the subject, a good, lively general one is Paul Tabori's *Pictorial History of Love,* Spring Books, 1968, etc., though its illustrations are all in black and white. Amongst the pictures it displays are the Elder Breughel's *Wedding Dance,* Pourbus's *Allegorical Love-Feast,* and the *Sleeping Venus* by Giogione.

(v). The audience should be encouraged to participate in the concert by joining in the performance of the simpler songs and rounds. Easy songs on the love theme are, inevitably, *Greensleeves* and the charming *Calino Custurame.* Of the rounds in this collection, *O My Love* is particularly easy, and, in fact, all but the nine-part round should be possible. If a screen and projector are available, a slide can be made of each round as a visual aid for the audience. It is advisable to make the audience rehearse in unison twice, and in performance, to make them sing the round in parts twice, causing them to end in a loud unison by repetition of the last line until all parts are home. The different sections of the audience can be reinforced by members of the choir singing either from the stage or from the auditorium. Rehearsing an audience for a round or song need take no more than two or three lighthearted and entertaining minutes of what is, after all, a concert mainly for their benefit.

6. Omitted stanzas of text. In four items, stanzas have been omitted from the body of the text. In the case of the first and the third, the setting apparently did not contain the additional stanzas. In the remaining two it was felt that including all verses might result in tedium in performance, but in any event, would cramp the underlay and take up valuable space which could otherwise be used for squeezing in another madrigal. To make the volume complete it was thought best to record them, nevertheless.

Mon Coeur

2. Banni j'en suis par faux semblant,
Mais pour nous voir encore ensemble,
Faut que me soyez ressemblant
De fermeté; car il me semble
Que quand faux rapport desassemble
Les amans qui sont assemblés,
Si ferme Amour ne les rassemble,
Sans fin seront desassemblés.

Come Again *(original verse 6 renumbered 3 in this edition)*

3. All the day
The sun that lends me shine
By frowns do cause me pine,
And feeds me with delay;
Her smiles my springs that make my joys to grow;
Her frowns the winters of my woe.

4. All the night
My sleeps are full of dreams,
My eyes are full of streams;
My heart takes no delight
To see the fruits and joys that some do find,
And mark the storms are me assigned.

5. Out alas!
My faith is ever true;
Yet she will never rue,
Nor yield me any grace.
Her eyes of fire, her heart of flint is made,
Whom tears nor truth may once invade.

Mas Vale Trocar *(original verse 6 renumbered 3 in this edition)*

3. La muerte es vitoria
Do bive afición,
Qu'espera aver gloria
Quien sufre pasión.
Mejor es prisión
De tales dolores
Qu'estar sin amores.

4. El qu'es más penado
Más goza d'amor,
Qu'el mucho cuidado
Le quita el temor.
Así qu'es mejor
Amar con dolores
Qu'estar sin amores.

5. No teme tormento
Quien ama con fe,
Si su pensamiento
Sin causa no fué.
Aviendo por qué,
Más vale dolores
Qu'estar sin amores.

So Wünsch Ich Ihr
(The underlay to the music forms the first stanza.)

2. In rechter Treu ist sie mir lieb,
Der ich mein Herz hab geben.
Zu dienen ihr ich mich stets üb,
Dieweil ich hab das Leben.
Dan sie hat mich
So herziglich
Mit ihrer Zucht gefangen.
Keins Menschen Freud
Mir Hoffnung geit,
Nach der mich tut verlangen.

3. Ohn alle Falsch will ich doch sein
Bis an meins Lebens Ende,
Gegen dir Allerliebsten mein,
Von der ich mich nit wende.
Mit Seufzen Klag,
Sich Nacht und Tag,
Mein hat mein Herz besessen,
Drum ich nun in
Dem Herzen brinn
Und fann ihr nicht vergessen.

チェスター社マドリガル楽譜シリーズ

このシリーズは、16世紀から17世紀初頭のヨーロッパのマドリガルと合唱曲を、目的別に集めたユニークなアルバムです。各巻はテーマ別に分けられ、第一巻は**動物**、第二巻は**愛と結婚**のシリーズになっています。各巻の解説にあるようにコンサートのプログラム作成にも便利です。

編成は混声四部合唱ですが、混声三部又は五部のものも若干含まれ、六部の曲もあります。

この曲集に入っているマドリガルは、最も有名でポピュラーなもの、魅力的で歌いやすいが余り知られていないもの等です。歌詞は、曲によってオリジナルの英語、イタリア語、フランス語、ドイツ語、及びスペイン語がついています。

チェスター社の**モテット楽譜シリーズ**と同様、この**マドリガル楽譜シリーズ**は演奏用、又は研究用に適するものとして作成されています。又、最も権威ある原典を資料にしていることは、音楽専門家にとって大変参考になります。

The Chester Books of Madrigals
Edited by Anthony G. Petti

Book 1: THE ANIMAL KINGDOM

	Composer	Title	Voices
1.	Jacob Arcadelt	*Il Bianco e Dolce Cigno*	**SATB**
2.	Adriano Banchieri	*Contrapunto Bestiale*	**SSATB**
3.	Orlando Gibbons	*The Silver Swan*	**SAATB**
4.	Josquin des Près	*El Grillo*	**SATB**
5.	Orlandus Lassus	*Audite Nova*	**SATB**
6.	Claude Le Jeune	*Petite Importune Mouche*	**SAT: SSATB**
7.	Lorenz Lemlin	*Der Gutzgauch*	**SSSATB**
8.	Claude Le Jeune	*Une Puce*	**SATB**
9.	Claudio Monteverdi	*Dolcissimo Usignolo*	**SSATB; solo ad lib.**
10.	Pierre Passereau	*Il est Bel et Bon*	**SATB**
11.	Thomas Ravenscroft	*The Three Ravens*	**SATB; solo ad lib.**
12.	Thomas Weelkes	*The Ape, the Monkey and Baboon*	**SABar.**
13.	Thomas Ravenscroft	Rounds from *Pammelia:*	
		(i) *New Oysters*	**3 voices**
		(ii) *The White Hen*	**4 voices**
		(iii) *The Old Dog*	**3 voices**
		(iv) *As I Me Walked*	**4 voices**
		(v) *Lady, Come Down and See*	**4 voices**
14.	Seventeenth Century Rounds:		
	(i) Anon.	*Well Rung, Tom*	**4 voices**
	(ii) Matthew White	*My Dame Hath a Lame Tame Crane*	**4 voices**
	(iii) Michael Wise	*A Catch on the Midnight Cats*	**3 voices**

Book 3: DESIRABLE WOMEN

	Composer	Title	Voices
1.	Anonymous (German)	*Traut Marle*	**SATB**
2.	Anonymous (Spanish)	*Marfira, Por Vos Muero*	**SATB**
3.	Anonymous (Spanish)	*Pase El Agoa, Ma Julieta*	**SATB**
4.	Jacob Arcadelt	*Margot Labourez Les Vignes*	**SATB**
5.	Jacob Arcadelt	*Carissima Isabella*	**SATB**
6.	Guillaume Costeley	*Perrette, Disait Jean*	**SATB**
7.	Giovanni Gastoldi	*Bellissima Mirtilla*	**SSATB**
8.	John Farmer	*Fair Phyllis*	**SATB**
9.	Orlandus Lassus	*Matona Mia Cara*	**SATB**
10.	Orlandus Lassus	*Vedi L'Aurora*	**SAATB**
11.	Thomas Morley	*No, No, No, No, Nigella*	**SSATB**
12.	Thomas Morley	*Said I That Amaryllis?*	**SSATB**
13.	John Wilbye	*Adieu, Sweet Amaryllis*	**SATB**
14.	Stephan Zirler	*Ach Gretlein*	**SATB**
15.	Seventeenth Century Rounds:		
	(i) Thomas Ravenscroft	*Go To Joan Glover*	**4 voices**
	(ii) Thomas Ravenscroft	*Joan, Come Kiss Me Now*	**3 voices**
	(iii) William Lawes	*Come, Amaryllis*	**4 voices**
	(iv) William Webb	*Good Susan*	**3 voices**
	(v) John Hilton	*Pretty Nan*	**3 voices**

Book 4: THE SEASONS

	Composer	Title	Voices
		Spring	
1.	Claude Le Jeune	*Revecy Venir Du Printemps*	**SMez.ATB & soli**
2.	Claudio Monteverdi	*O Primavera*	**SMez.ATB**
3.	Thomas Morley	*Springtime Mantleth Every Bough*	**SABar.**
4.	John Hilton	*Now That The Spring*	**3-part round**
		Maytime	
5.	Thomas Morley	*Now Is The Month of Maying*	**SATTB**
6.	Clément Jannequin	*A Ce Joli Mois*	**SATB**
7.	Michael Praetorius	*Herzlich Tut*	**SATB**
8.	John Hilton	*Come Let Us All Amaying Go*	**3-part round**
		Summer and Autumn	
9.	John Hilton	*Now Is The Summer Springing*	**SST**
10.	Anonymous (English)	*Summer Is Icumen In*	**4-12 part round**
11.	Melchior Franck	*Kommt, Ihr G'Spielen*	**SATB**
12.	Ippolito Baccusi	*Ben Sei Felice Autunno*	**SMez.ATB**
		Winter	
13.	Thomas Weelkes	*To Shorten Winter's Sadness*	**SSATB**
14.	Caspar Othmayr	*Der Winter Kalt Ist Vor Dem Haus*	**SATB**
15.	Philippe de Monte	*Ceda Ogni Altra Stagion*	**SSATB**
16.	John Hilton	*Arm, Arm, Arm*	**3-part round**
		Love and the Seasons	
17.	Jacob Arcadelt	*L'Hiver Sera Et L'Eté Variable*	**SATB**
18.	Thomas Morley	*April Is In My Mistress' Face*	**SATB**
19.	Thomas Ravenscroft (ed.)	*Oaken Leaves*	**3-part round**
20.	Michael Praetorius	*Der Winter Ist Ein Strenger Gast*	**SATB**

CHESTER MUSIC

Printed and bound in Great Britain by
Caligraving Limited Thetford Norfolk